I WORE MY BLACKEST HAIR

I Wore My Blackest Hair

poems by

CARLINA DUAN

Little
a

Text copyright © 2017 by Carlina Duan
All rights reserved.

Published by Little A, New York

www.apub.com

Amazon, the Amazon logo, and Little A are trademarks of Amazon.com, Inc., or its affiliates.

ISBN-13: 9781503941977
ISBN-10: 1503941973

Cover design by Faceout Studio

Cover illustration by Hannah Perry

Printed in the United States of America

For my parents,
whom I love

CONTENTS

& for every country that i've lost
i make another & i make another

—Safia Elhillo

I WORE MY BLACKEST HAIR

Father's chopsticks crashed. He threw them. He dared me to say it again. *I _____ you,* I said. Sister closed the door. I walked away from the bowls, pressed my cheek to the piano. In front of me, black keys shinier than a fingernail. I'd forgotten how to play. My hands were soft. Father could not believe he had raised such a daughter. *Get the hell out of my house.* His face did not quiver, only his hands. Dinner with Father: I left; I did not leave. On the driveway, a black stone sat. Father coughed a mouthful of rice. Chinese in his fists. *Shǎ guā gūniang! Shǎ.* Midnight, alone in my room, I Google translated. *Idiot girl. Idiot.* In the dream, Rage took my tongue and flung it on a fishing line. Another Self watched as the hook laid into me, robbing my mouth. *I _____ you.* Out loud: I blued, horrible with regret. He broke a bowl. Girl. *Gūniang.* He said get out. Dinner in Michigan: my father, extraordinary and old and Chinese. I am a lion with a black mane, tearing my teeth on the piano bench. My English is hot, pursuing me with a gun.

PLEDGE ALLEGIANCE

my mother is not
from your country
filled with chocolates
and rain.

don't ask me
where my solitude
comes from—
in this country I know
we floss our teeth.

in this country I know
how to swim, how to part
my lips. what's black,
what's bent. what's
not mine to touch.

salt sparkles
on sidewalks of
clean snow. in
this country
my lungs
are strong. my elbows,
sharp: I get that
from my mother.

we do not pour soy
sauce on our rice.
we do not eat our
cheeseburgers
with quiet hands;
we toast white
breads and smash
their faces thick
with butter.

my mother
is not from your
country, and I am
her daughter.
don't ask me
what it's like
being small
and Chinese.

I have Tupperware
and eat almonds
I have pride: warm
and plump,
like a moon.

my mother
does not own a
Laundromat or
a take-out restaurant;
she waters orchids

and doesn't look
your president
in the eye.

my mother is not
from your country,
and I am not
ashamed.

I slip my hands
through her
wise hair,

and keep.

WHAT YOU LOOKIN' AT, CHINK?

she yelled out the car window. I clutched
the soft drink in my yellow hand,
turned paw at the intersection. bodies
brushed past me. the straw stuck
ghostly to my snout. the light flashed red
then green. she squeezed past the bike
lane. I took a sip, and the cold shot down
a throat, wetted my whiskers. inside
a furry ear, the word *CHINK* swerved
and thrashed.

> the Chink is a mammal who loves dirt
> and kernels of white rice. the Chink
> is a mammal who sharpens pencils,
> twitches beneath a blank sky.

> the Chink flashes her a look like a switch-

> blade, eats muffins,

> drives at precise speed
> limits. the Chink clenches
> and unclenches a mouth.

> beware of the Chink: how it bites.

WHEN I BOILED THE CORN

I thought first about minnows

> & my father's brow lifting each
> time he drew flights of fish
> on blank paper—fins glinting
> like proper coins. he would draw
> them in his highest anger, Mandarin
> & English drilling currents through
> his mouth:

fuck / man
warrior / pig

> words he couldn't catch
> with a rod—or his hands.

the corn came in husks,
which I tore off.

> my father's tongue was not
> torn but rather steamed: English
> vowels & consonants hitting hot
> air, pink roof of the mouth, hissed
> & flung out at the gas station,
> at the university lab. *This is what*
> *we're going to do today. Do you un-*
> *derstand?* English bolted itself

to my throat, and my father
did not move, watched me eat
yogurt & ride a scooter 'til the English
battery powered my jaw, my hands. my
father drew fish and did not flick
the switch; alphabet chafed my thighs
& moved me, up and down a street
where I owned syllables untouched
by my father:

gold / good / god
home / help / him / amen

when I first called my father an ass-
hole in English he did not stand up
but shook in his chair, & that is when
I knew the knife had cinched a fish
eye, its round & simple jelly, lifted
toward the ceiling, no hope or muscle
left, no nothing at all.

everywhere around me: kernels
of corn so hot to swallow.

before I reach the lid
there is the steam
and a crystallized sheet
of brown water at the bottom
of the pan, yellow ears
wet & pronounced. I

think of how the Chinese
character for *loss*
is one I must memorize
from the Internet, so
come dinnertime I say
nothing, press my fingers
into the pan, & this
is how I burned
the corn. how
I fed my father.

AMENORRHEA

that was the month when the heart made its earnest pelting
and began to break the dishes in the sink one
by one
when the car backed into the driveway with dim
red light and Mom filed all the medical papers
into plastic bins labeled with my name

I mispronounced the word *gynecologist*
stretched it tight-
ly against my mouth

I haunted high school bathrooms
each morning with a cotton bag of pads
touched the dried drops
of other girls' blood on toilet seats
color of roses and jam

when I shoved Pop

Tarts down my throat in calculus class and Adam said
something about tapioca   how I didn't hear him
thought about thickness and clots clouds of blood

in the middle of the month I got my period
the red on my panties sticky like pudding I
unpeeled the pad I said *Girl*   *I am a girl again thank*
god

after seven months &   the boxes of white pills
the dry underwear   the radiology department
the doctors touching   my abdomen
                              Does it hurt here when I press does it hurt

after all we carried into the waiting room
tea leaves   & mints   cysts
their thumbs
in between my legs as if plowing   for gold I said *Please please* until

suddenly I   popped
and the blood

                              rushed in
                              wet   final

                              prize.

WHEN ALL YOU WANT

is the piano again, and Mrs. Liu with her
handsome mouth saying, *Wrong. E minor.*
Do it again, your hands flashing against
the keyboard, dreaming about cool bodies
of water. your mom peering anxiously
from the window. the boy in the next
practice room playing violin with
his neck, the Creme Saver candies
in Mrs. Liu's mouth: clack, suck, clack,
again—here go all the noises you love.

you are seven, and you do believe
in toucans, in being the older sister.
you do believe in rainbow bills. you
want to kiss each of the keys: black
polish, white, black, but Mrs. Liu says,

FOCUS—

on the piano bench, you pop open
your beak. slam your fists into the half
notes, the whole notes; the feathers on
your waist begin to trill. you imagine
the insides of the piano as a zoo, caging
schools of fish, a river. there are pink
skies in your hands. you spread them
across the keyboard. your knuckles

become ten white moons; the keys
howl: hungry wolves.

the piano is sometimes
a younger sister, lifting its face
to you. it must. with your fingers
you are brassy and mean. sonatas
leak everywhere, hatching A-flats
and D notes and birds and birds
and birds, birds. your talons
press the gold pedal,
making the room echo.
Mrs. Liu tells your mom you
should practice more. you pat
the keys with a wing; she
swallows a Creme Saver.
you whir a tail, and flit
across the keys.

CALUMET

I was lonely. I disinfected the sink.
I spoke to boys in orange jumpsuits

who were not allowed to shake my hand.
for Halloween, I brought in milk chocolate

bars. the security guard told them,
One. You can only have one,

and the sugar flashed quickly
on their thick boy tongues.

they asked me who I was,
what was I doing. I was lonely.

I disinfected the sink. I drew curly
letters on a board and passed out pencils.

their eyes hit the ceiling. they said,
No, no, we don't write—then wrote

about matchsticks and daughters,
roofs and car tires, sticky sugar

in cinnamon rolls. they wrote. & through
the doors, in came their old loves, wearing

jeans and red sneakers. in came bed frames,
sports magazines, nail clippers. in came brothers,

the feeling of arm hair against arm hair
and baby's wrists, fire, Drake lyrics,

cups of ice cream, dizzy spins in
the front seat of a black car. then in

came my ghosts, too: pattering
across the room, arms sagging

with all that had flocked
and gone. the boys said,

We don't write—the room
filled and filled.

by the time I left, the tables teemed
with a million basketballs,

wisps of candy, threads
of lightning, loss.

they scribbled on tall sheets
with their pencils. they did not cry.

every day, they blazed the old ghosts
into everything. when I left, they kept

their papers. they did not ask
me to come back.

WHAT I'VE LOST

teeth. metallic parts of head-
phones, bad machinery. sticks
of lead. loves I once pressed
my lips to, firm and hard, on
their whole precious throats.
entire countries streaked
with black pepper,
entire countries
bleating with the creamy milk
of goats. it is absolute: this loss.
rivers and eyelashes. onions
waggling their roots. what I
will never know: new sisters
and stones curled into the center
of a palm. what I've missed:
kernels of corn, kettles of water.

I am lonely, in my lonely chest.

birds traipse out of windows. flags
lift their red and floppy throats.
cars shout; I will never hear them.

I want to catch so much of this earth
on the gentle tongue, but
outside: there is only snow.
and inside: there is only muscle.

only what I can give and flex—
which is to say, inside: there is
a moon in me, a heart
that swamps and swamps.

today: oil and vessel. turnips
I fried for dinner. joy I got
from touching a friend's humble
face. the monthly blood. the honest
stutter. what I place my paws on:
only rain, only squares of papaya,
and the hundred lives in me:
tender, eager to sprout.

MORNING COMES, I AM SHINY WITH IT

in memory of Wàipó

—*i.*

in my dream last night you wore a boa constrictor
around your neck. I touched the scales, sharp green
and slick in my hands. you opened your mouth
while the creature swam around and around
your throat. on your wrist, a thread of blood
beneath skin: bluish, strong. we watched
the night swell. in my dream we stood in a parking
garage. I cried while animals slipped
into you: woodpeckers and poisonous
frogs; orange clownfish, too.

—*ii.*

as a girl, I widened my mouth. you fed
me water chestnuts from a spoon
and drew eyebrows on my Lucy doll
with a black pencil. *Āiya,* you said,
clenching a tongue, and I watched
you press into the face, making lines
where there were none. this was before
the first stroke, before the second,
before I visited in summers and Dà Yí caught
your drool in a tin pan. before your arms
gave out, you gutted a melon with a broad knife.
juice and seed slathered our chins, I flexed

a leg, calling you Brave. you asked me if it
was true: in Michigan, could I sometimes see
eagles? did I sometimes eat strawberries? were
there—or weren't there—patches
of dumb yellow stars?

—*iii.*

when you died, I called home from a pay phone in Spain,
where a man tried to sell me ice cream in a pink cooler
and I fended him off by mouthing, *Muerte, abuela,*
muerte, away from the receiver. my Pain was glassy
and slow. in my dream, I tried to tell you about it:
the crackle, the hush, my mom's long fever, but you
opened your mouth and out flew a pelican, out flew
a rainbow trout. a turtle waddled across your tongue,
as if to say everything you could not: *There, there now.*
Child. Girl. Small animal heart. Bark, bleat. Bray. You won't
get her back. the turtle climbed over my toes,
and from your lips, out flew the hornets, out flew
the killer whales. *We have her now. We have her now,*
they said, clenching their jaws, hatching eggs
across the floors. *There, there.* they
flashed their stunning and terrible teeth.
morning cracked, bright and desperate
and small. the animals latched onto you:
This one, she is ours now, they said, kissing me
with their snouts before the sun broke, and I
woke up, my face shiny against a pillow.

EAST ANN

the morning I eat the rest of
Jean's muffins, the radiator
snaps its throat and I shove
blades of bread in the toaster.

the mild sun. the mild dog hairs
on my lap, the blackened TV
uncrackling in the foyer.

in August, when we brought
the couch in, Alex bent his hip
while Jean cooked red
peppers on the stove.

I said, *Are you sure
it'll fit?* and Alex said,
*We have to try. I mean
we have to.*

now this house has a couch
we don't sit on, and Jean keeps
the butter out on the table
in the winter. the radiators
whistle and pop and remind
me of my feet beneath water.

Jasmine comes over and says,
Have you ever been snorkeling?
I say, *No,* and she tells me there
are fish whose bodies arc
wild with rainbows.
the front porch is rain
and mint, a Bic lighter.
there are no fish
in our neighborhood,
but there is a seafood market.
in summers: my gills, my open
mouth, the neighbor's small dog
peeing in the brush.

in summers: Jean smokes
with her hair in a ponytail,
and I think about all the heat-
splash, what nerve
it took to get us here.

strain and mattress and all
the soft bodies we love,
bumping Wu-Tang and bare
kneed at our dinner table.

when Aaron comes home
in December we sit at
the wobbly table across
from each other and eat
carrots from a plastic bag.

I can tell he loves me, because
he doesn't look at the cracked
ceiling and eats baby carrot
after baby carrot and touches
the tip of my head.

when our dishwasher breaks,
we drink orange juice from
a flower vase, and I
snore in my sleep
and dream about
wonder and shoulder blades
and milk. I used to roller-
skate when my feet
were tinier and I loved
a different house
with green shutters.

most mornings, I wake
and wipe my neck
with paper towels in the dark.

most mornings, I dump
sugar cubes into the orange
mug and scratch my unwashed
hair.

LITTLE SISTER, AMERICAN GIRL

We mooned all over this house:
carpets, shiny jars of olives, hose water,
plots of sand. Spider plants sprouted
against tiles; against floors we ate
ice cream. I fed you often. Thought
I wasn't good enough to be
yours. Once you slipped and cracked
forehead against stairwell, and *Oh,* Mom said, *oh XIĔ, oh BLOOD,*
oh XIĂO
MÈIMEI. Look at your XIĂO
MÈIMEI, and a coil of red braided
your precious hair. Oh ambulance
in a blank country of collars
and fists. In this house, we swam.
When I came home from school
after beating up Lawrence
for calling me *SMALL EYES,*
you were the one I told my secrets
to. How I fluttered my black eyelashes.
How I smashed. To replace the
languages our mom spoke, we
smoked up our Chinese with blond
dolls, our new knees. American girls.
Chocolate and cream and violence
'til we ran into stairwells
and walls. we were told,
Quiet, XIĂO SHĒNGYĪN, and

used our chopsticks to stir cake
batter. to our mom and her bamboo
slippers, we said, *Please.* Swallowing
on sticky throats, we said, *Can't.*

GAME BOY ADVANCE

hover in the dumbstruck night.
milk in lonely cups, video games,
sister's pink forehead shining
in the dark. her spit, starred.
too embarrassed to ask her boss
for a lunch break, she eats
homemade edamame
at a Starbucks, four
hours after her shift—
Don't tell Mom.
napkins, blood
orange juicing her
hands. mouth round,
a leash. what she'll do
for minimum wage.
small animals flashing
across her screen.
night in our jaws,
in our teeth, until I grind.
moon flashing
like a white rumor
until I snap, call her
a child, swerve and yell
in her bed. *I don't like
to see you working
so hard.* I push against
her elbow; our cheeks

touch. she says
nothing. presses
the "A" button. kills
an animal mercilessly
with her thumb.

LATCHKEY

when Ache comes in,
she uses the garage door
& arches her back, reaching
for the spare key. her shoes
are blue. the air conditioner
hisses. she brushes our hair
with the tight, noiseless comb,
and our legs gallop on
the water bed. Ache tells us
about oysters, calcium, underwater
shells that pump open like
umbrellas. she rubs vanilla
balm on my lower lip.
my knee hurts. outside, amid
bleached grass: we swim and we
swim. Ache opens a package
of Oreos and looks at us
expectantly. we eat, mash. two
hours later I throw up, and Ache
loses the slip of paper with our
mother's phone number
scratched in purple pen.
Ache says an emergency is
no small thing. in Ache's
bag rests a tiny box of green-
tea mints, a postcard of
a sperm whale. I win

an entire card game;
we do not celebrate.
in high heat, I pass out
on the bed. Ache wets
a cloth for my head
and hums, her tongue
a nervous, thin fish.
before she is paid in
cash and leaves the
house full of swollen
fruits, the scent of disinfectant
and Hi-C, and cartoons
in her body, Ache
watches me sleep.

BELIEF

believe in the mosquito net: black wires catching
black wings, knotting them into fists, livid

bumps darting across the shoulder as you
scratch. across the street, a boy tosses a pear core

out the open window. believe in this, too: the pear,
its green body, its arc through

a cloud of gnats and wind until it lands on
pavement, tossing its juice onto a woman's

ankle. so believe in that ankle. its slow glide. its
hairs riding the leg: a history of razors and creamy

soaps. believe in low-rise jeans and buttons, thigh skin
stretched politely across pink muscle, entire leg

and knee and foot taught to stamp down dirt
while wearing cotton, wearing dark stains

of grass. believe in grass—where corn grows. where
pear seeds grow. an ant grows, weaves plots

of sand into tunnels and hills. believe in hills
and bellies, black hair. your sister's eyelashes as she

glances down at circles of honey ham
and your mother calling, *Chī fàn le! Chī*

fàn le! in her stickiest throat. and birds pumping
past the chilled window. and hammers kissing your

bedroom wall. and crumbs of bread
erased by brooms. and the house fire

that will someday erase the boy who dropped
the pear, pulsing its sweet juice all across

a sidewalk—though you don't
know this yet, age sixteen and still a child

who believes in the light curving fast
beyond the bus stop, the heart starting

its luscious whir as you pedal your legs past
the tree dusty with magnolia blossoms, past

the boy's blue house, past the entire
avenue, say you won't look back. believe, then,

in the mosquito: how it begins to take
your blood—heat and ghost and age and itch

as you press the net to your temples
and scratch in wild belief while

outside, leaves darken, insects
bite, and you smash a body

with the back
of your palm.

IT IS NOT ENOUGH

I wrestle with plastic bottles and fall asleep in cars.

my aunt touches a lemon tree, hands me scissors.

briskly, we cut. outside, tiny stems roll over tiny dirt.

I open my throat; rain falls in. clouds of milk fall in.

late nights I brush my teeth and stretch.

I love a friend with muddy elbows,

who keeps his hair oily and long.

once, he asked for a hair band, then nested

his hands into mine over the cotton bed.

the grass in this state is skinny and mean.

somewhere, police cars flash, pollute my body

with red and blue stars. somewhere, brothers

are tear gassed. we wear our bright American tongues.

a boy is shot. see his purple wrists.

see mine, outstretched beneath a sheen of blue water.

in another state, my friend raises a sign.

somebody punches

a stopwatch.

FRACTIONS, 1974

—i.

in the kitchen, my mother and her sister
talk in tiny whispers. a cultural revolution.
spirals of teeth. mouths centered into Os
like slow red pearls. by the sink, a fruit fly
whines, and my mother cinches the ribbon
of her dress, bites into a cucumber.
teaches her sister fractions—
all they haven't yet swallowed: Chinese
girls with flags pinned to their bags, Chinese
girls in love with the swell of onions
and moons. milk is measured out through
ration cards; a neighborhood rooster chases
their skirt hems.

years from now, we cackle in our throats.

in the capital, the windows are dirty with stars.
as the chairman lifts his hand to speak, a needle
punctures a strip of muslin cloth.

in the kitchen, my mother slips pills of rice
into tin cups, casts thin glances at
her sister. halves and wholes.
thirds and fourths. someday, American
daughters will speak the language
in sections—

—ii.

  a is for *apple*; *b* is for *bitch*

—iii.

once I called my mother *bitch*,
and she said, *BITCH. Shì shénme?*
WHAT IS THAT? teeth crackling
against lip until I saw her: a girl
again, splitting onions by
the sink.

I said, *MOM. MOM.*

while she called me

Nǚ'ér,
nǚ'ér.

I was her American
daughter, my tongue

my hardest muscle

forced to swallow
a muddy alphabet.

each night my mother taught me
Chinese myths, fractions. we
watched the night crawl. bagged
into blackness, our tongues traced
English and Chinese,

English and Chinese,
two throats.

YOUR MOM TELLS YOU TO
STOP WRITING ABOUT RACE

so you punch buttons. so you side-part
your hair. so you flip through TV channels
and watch monkeys howl with their bare
monkey lips, so you are reminded of your
father. a gas station, a black nozzle, a man
in the adjacent car pinching his eyes, his
wide blue face: telling you to go back
home. you draw shark teeth on your
American culture homework. you raise
your hand in class. your house becomes
a zoo filled with peaches, watercolor
roosters. each year, you walk and you
walk and your feet perform quietly
in the grass. everybody asks you for
tricks, their name in black calligraphy.
everybody coos and coos. there
are cages, and there are your eyes.
there are your ten thousand days, eggy
and glorious, stuck through the teeth of
a comb. your skin is sticky and yellow.
your tongue is ancient and sweet. when
a boy plumps his lip on your throat
and asks you to say *something dirty*
in CHINESE, you flip the sheets
and bite down, tasting trouble
and rage. in the kitchen, alone,

you devour a pickle. your white
classmate sees you. does not.
white men claim you. do not.
you are small, fierce, and evil: with
two palms and a chest. there are
boxes made for you to check. *Chinese /
American. Chinese / American.*
your mom calls. she tells you to stop
writing about race. *You could get
shot,* she says. so you yank your hair
into a knot at the back of your neck.
so you cinch your belt tight
at the waist.

I WASN'T JOKING

I got a collarbone. I got
an untidy mouth. I got
a scalp where rain darts.
watch my palms chase
through the head's black
gully—in each arm-
pit I grow and grow
the flossy hairs. in each
armpit I sweat, sprout.
I got a yodel in me; watch
me flex. precise. watch
the pinkest muscle: won't
give up my tongue for no
one—how it slices
and drums. in a dream
men told me I was small
and what did I know,
woman with modest toes
and knees. when they
patted me on the head I
slashed the dirt; I slashed
the gladiola, nipples flowered
like purple planets. all my
hair chirped; I opened
my mouth and let my
hundred teeth show:
saliva, gums. canines

glinted, flashed
the flash of rivers.
when I bit my bottom
lip they said,

     Oh,

and I turned
vicious: girl
stroking the earth
with two biceps. let
no one take my
tongue. I got a yodel
in me, won't back down
without parting my lips,
wet and eager
for the flight—

AUBADE FOR ANGEL ISLAND, CHINA COVE

In 1905, construction of an Immigration Station began in the area known as China Cove. The facility, primarily a detention center, was designed to control the flow of Chinese into the country, since they were officially not welcomed with the passage of the Chinese Exclusion Act of 1882.

—Angel Island Conservancy

I press my mouth

into a pink pistol

clang my teeth

into a galaxy of

in early light. catch
a moth darkening its wings

atop the window. floorboards, coils of
black hair. all I want to smuggle, want to shut,

into: apples, allegiance. detained for days and days,
days and days. I plant my names on the walls. drop

dirty necks, combs. they call me *foreigner.* call me
Chinaman, slice me up with all their pinks: all their

tongue, tongue:

lift my lips

to pummel—

lift my throat

to begin.

English teeth and English hands. I place my own on
the windows. cool air, an anthem. a throat to clear.

in this country, with its hinged doors and coins,
they call me *Slit Eyes*. wait for me

I strike back. in my country: men tuck their teeth into pears
and rain. in my country: I torch the moon,

beneath its blanched belly of white. Chinaman. I
open the door. I rock the ship. I eye; I water. I stay

EVERYTHING'S A FLY

in this house. & my vision's
blurry. it smells the wild smell
of feet. I spread lotion on my face:
moony & white. when I was small,
my father put Pond's cream
on his hands. scent of linen
& something sharp: birds' nests,
maybe, or wings. my father
never read me stories, but he
leaned in & I sucked in many
breaths, holding in oceans, open
doors, wind, sweet.

I believe in my father.

presidential teeth, elongated
and gapped. when I stick a finger
through his scalp I find stars.
I bury them back between
dandruff and salt. I come
from a lineage of men who draw
scores of bright fish on their palms
and refuse to call it easy. they
do not pet my head. when they
high-five me, I meet the current,
wash my neck. shake my fins.

I am the daughter of
black tide / *an immigrant.*

where my father lives, I protect.

we swim and we swim.

flies poke their bodies through
& through, humming
the plumpest black. I vote
for my father to kill
them, but he turns to me,
hands me the swatter—

                    This is your country—

tells me to strike quick.

there is an entire liquid
nation in his face and no-
where to admit what I
fear. some day the president
might hurt him, or lie, or
dismiss: my *bàba* who
cleans my passport with
alcohol wipes and stands
in the frozen-foods aisle
for minutes, carrying
the fruit sorbet in his arms
as he would a soft child.

in the kitchen
the flies descend upon
a perfect peach,
and my father stands
in the corner, waiting,
so *kill, kill,* I do

                and I do.

AT THE SUSHI RESTAURANT
HE CALLS HIMSELF A GRINGO

snaps the wooden chopsticks in half,
and asks me what to do next.

I place the shrimp politely in
a mouth. grease swims and sizzles.

he watches but does not
follow, his arm hairs lay flat and soft

on skin. he places
the napkin in a lap,

winds up a wrist, eyes the strips of
fish: pink and slim and wet. ginger

toughens my breath. I breathe out;
he breathes in. *The texture,*

he says. *The texture is like a rubber
band.* I chew; meat snaps

between my teeth. he says, *I don't
know about raw fish. Are you sure*

it's sanitary? and I smack my
lips: daring him to come closer.

he asks me what
to do. I say, *Eat, Eat.*

ANN ARBOR, MICHIGAN • GENERATION 1

on my tongue: clove and ginger. spit, a shimmer.
flecks of black pepper. in another country,
friends I love grow out their hair.
in another country, my grandfather's ashes
press primly beneath the ground. I am lonely
here, when all around me, lemongrass grows.
out of my throat, noises swim. I howl and I
howl. a woman calls me by another woman's
name. *Franny,* she says. I am not Franny:
I am brick, elbow. with my mouth I
swallow wrinkles of light. in my armpits
there are clumps of black hair. men call me;
I do not call them back. I tilt my chin;
I slice a lime: firm green disc. I hold it nicely
in my hands. it is the lunar year. there is
a gold moon. I check my horoscope.
I check the news: bullets. ghosts that trail
the dirt, disguised as cups of milk, sparrows.
I check my sister's face; this is what wonder
must be. filled with holes. a moon, a gold rush.
pigtails. once, my Chinese grandfather died.
once, I barked: a wild animal. once,
a man said, *This isn't a cultural study. This is
a literary study,* and I touched the tips of my
hair. I slammed my face into the
window of a school bus, where, in the back,
boys chanted, *WHO LET THE DOGS OUT?*

WHO, WHO, WHO, WHO? and the glass cooled
me, my stern wrist, my sterner heart. every day
there was a wall. there was a wallet. there was
my mother packaging *miàntiáo* by the sink.
breath in the morning. breath in the afternoon.
the way history comes back to haunt me with
a plump fist. the way my mouth, a cave, opened
and closed. my family told me, *Do not forget it,*
and I did not. my love for lamps, my love for
noodles. my hurt when they lashed my name
with their throats. *CHINA. CHINA. YOU
EAT DOGS.* the wheels on the bus
go round and round. we lurch we lurch.
we spit we spit. we remember our names,
carved sharply into the walls.

USIS • ANGEL ISLAND, CALIFORNIA • GENERATION 0

With little to do on an isolated island, some detainees passed the time by expressing their feelings in poetry that they brushed or carved into the wooden walls. . . . Poems lost to layers of paint over the years, were unknowingly, in 1931–32, documented by two immigrants, Smiley Jann and Tet Yee, who copied the poetry while they awaited ruling of their cases.

—Angel Island Conservancy

we remember to carve
our names sharply
into the walls.

they spit they spit,

    China(man),   China(man),   you eat dogs?

lashed by memory—noodles
wet and furiously long.

I did not forget. the way my mouth
caved. the way I swung, then
missed, the way I bunched a fist.

there was a window, a wall. there was
a pane of glass. my stern heart cooled,
then chanted, *LET ME OUT LET ME*—
a small dog in a smaller cage. I slammed
my face into the tips of my hair. a man
said, *Specimen, Chinese . . . Isn't that nice?*
I barked: a wild animal. with my mouth
I swallowed wrinkles of light.

there was a lunar year, then
another. the news filled me
with holes. in my armpits there
were clumps of black hair. in me
there was pain, a gold rush.

in another country, I held it all
nicely in my hands: black pepper,
hair, lemongrass, my sisters.

here, I am lonely:
I howl and I howl,

who let the dogs out?
who, who, who,

who?

MOON PULL

I don't want to hear the physics behind everything I do. I know it's there, lurking like a greyhound moon in between my toothpaste, my thumbs, the body's scribble. there are skin cells on my jeans. there is plurality in the way I leave myself behind. I am gone by the thousands: saliva, nail, stripe of hair; see me seeping into the dirt. into the water. the young earth had no moon. all of it a rogue planet, caught between diamond and dust. today, the moon pulls our water up, into tide & marathon of tide, pulls tree sap, puddles, my spit. the moon is mysterious and full of a liquid core; it is draining me down every night. I am a child when I look at the moon. it festers handsomely in the sky; I am small, small. I am small. I want to touch the moon on its limp face; physics won't let me. I want to be everywhere the moon is; physics says nothing about drought— what to do about restless bone. water tastes differently every time I go to a new fountain. a new house. I stay suspended beneath the moon and all its tantrums. the moon quivers, won't look me in the eye. it is the same every day. if the moon's gravity pulls on water to make tides, I want to be pulled, too. every wet slice of me rummaging for moon over my driveway, my window. I want to orbit around my house. the diameter of the moon is too big for me to skim over. its gravity is only one-sixth that of the earth. the moon glazes its rocks, rotates and pulls, pulls with craters and throats. every day, the light dries out. I am thirsty from below.

I RUN AND I RUN AND I

don't stop
my foot catches
on wires and grass
at the farmers' market
I pass the honey man with his fingers
plugged in a jar I purr sweet
I wave a hand I run and the
cars honk their small throats I am
tired of waiting at the intersections
where mailboxes bang inside sheets of rust
I run and sandwiches dress
in mayonnaise then strut down aisles
of wax paper *It's spring* I think *Every-
body is attractive* I run to the river
see the dogs bark in gruff tongues
want to pet their furs but I run
spy couples kissing on the neck *Oh*
I think but the breeze shuts me up I run
and doors bang at the hinges
waiters sniff
my sister seals paper
in graphite with her left hand
chocolate pops into the oven and
everything smells lusty and mahogany while
a pacifier trumpets in the dust but
I run I run I am full speed and whirring
   and too fast in love

THEN I WOKE UP IN YOUR BED

pretending to sleep while the fan, on & on,
hissed. in fifth grade, I did a school project
on oceans and threw my hands into clay,
shaping fins, a narwhal's tusk.
at night, into your back, I threw my hands,
composing water: coral reefs, sand, the lone
light of an anglerfish. at night, you pressed a
mouth to my neck. navel, blue current, vein,
I know nothing about the ocean: only gills—
only breath, only hands, mustering the tide
in your skin. mid-dream, you stirred; I lay
sharked, sharp in love. in your bed, morning
leaked across your chin. I threw my hands
into cotton sheets, hot and hot and arched,
while next to me, the hiss, the fan, a body
of water slept.

SEVERED

after you left the country, there was an oil spill
off the Louisiana coast. birds coiled their wings.
fish strummed through the water, then died.

in the kitchen, I placed pickles on squares of
whole-grain bread. outside, puddles
slid in rainbow grease.

somewhere, you pushed a hand into the cash
register. swallowed a melatonin pill, sucked in
scents of gasoline, grass. on another continent,

you flashed your knees. off the coastline,
a wing puckered black. we were too far away
to notice. I wished, many times, for your hand.

after you left the country, a small field of silence.
artichokes locked inside a can. dead amphibians
and my small chest, ghosting and fuming

after you. meanwhile, Ache smoothed its fingers
on the nape of my neck. told me to keep quiet, tread
water. forget the leathery strap of your name.

HERE I GO, TORCHING

he came over. asked, *What are you?*
I said it out loud. he said, *Oh,*
disappointed. *I thought you*
were Malaysian. I turned small
and wiped my ash mouth. his
tasted like green onions, lampshades.
light gone bad. he said, *Konnichiwa,*
then kissed me 'til I twanged. 'til
the muscle in my face snapped.
freckles all over his arm: small
brown rhymes. my body:
bilingual threat. muscle
in my tongue, in each slice
I speak. black plains of hair.
plain of mouth, of meat. he
pushed up my shirt, ricochet.
gunpowder teeth, he wanted neither
of my tongues. just gold hoops
in my ears. metal in the tank,
in the bed. I'm Chinese; see me
and my pulled muscle. see him
and his snapped trigger. our sputter
and splash into the night. glow of my
own simple skin. quietly, he stayed.

I didn't speak.

HEY, MAN

don't let yourself in.
see me, black hair.
pimple. pink moon.
I open my mouth and
call it a *GOOD DAY*—did I
startle you? I got
a crackle in my
fist. see me
prickle, then spark.
see me guzzle the
wind, 'cause I can.
you wanna pet
my hair? purr?
OH, you wanna kiss?
I got a good fight.
I got cuss words
packed in my sleeve:
BANG, BANG.
don't rest;
don't mistake
me for a soft woman,
a shy mouth—
I can lash like the
hot, hot rain. I stick
a dahlia between my
teeth, call it
NUTRITION;

I bite and hoof
and gnash. hey,
man. I got a
brain to unbutton.
got muscle taut
and strong
in my chest.
don't you
come into this
house with
your fly unzipped;
this is your first
warning. get out.

SHUT DOWN

the night I decided to leave you,
the government shut down.

my knees were cold.
I drank tap water and listened to jazz.

somewhere: eighty thousand federal workers
furloughed. a million asked to work

without pay. I poured olive oil
into a pan; my black hair crackled blacker.

on television: the president
& his moist lip.

outside, a truck flared its wheels.
I undressed and watched my bare stomach

bloat beneath a light
bulb. quietly, & curried with rage,

I sliced
a plum.

AT THE PARTY

my sister leans over the banister while a girl
passes out beers & sealed packets of Sour
Patch Kids. Eliza is dancing. I watch her
elbows jerk, knees simple & strong, face
knifing into mine, *Hello hello* as the radio
wails and from it: songs about asterisks
& hairy fists. by the back door
Terence pats my arm, says, *I like your*
necklace. So good to see you, 'til I turn
this way and that—catching the light on my
teeth: smelling turnips & sparklers, the wet
dollar bill lumped inside my jeans.

before the party, my mom calls. I am flossing
my teeth. her voice brays across the phone;
words gallop through me. I hold the lipstick: a
shade named Creature. my mouth shape-
shifts into a purple cloud. on the phone
my mother's voice lifts its hooves &
rams over my throat: *Hello hello?*
Do you hear me?
  Tumor,
tumor. *Your aunt has*
a tumor.
Do you hear me? she says

—everybody's skin looks so clean.

at the party I am too old; I touch
my neck. I touch Terence's face, touch
a silver beer can, a windowpane,
a potted plant spilling tender leaves
onto the striped couch. my mouth
begins to weep a purple weep, firm
and bricklike with knowing.

she'll die. or she won't. & inside
the carriage house, Eliza will
dance with her knees. close
to me, a couple makes out, her
lips puddling into his nose, a face.
everything gives way to light.
I touch the fold of skin on my
ankle, struck by all the salt water
in me—a body built by other
bodies, precious & flailing &
mean. at the party we hum
rock songs, & boys in bad hair-
cuts shuffle, don't sleep. my
aunt grows a vicious patch
of tissue on her neck.
the doctors haven't yet
said, *Cancer.* if they do,
I won't pick up. the tongue
inside my jaw is smashed fruit,
unworkable; I open my mouth
& am ashamed.

PACKING LUNCH ON ANN STREET

red and purple candies spill into a plastic bag.
cherry, grape: pour liquid in my mouth.
through cavities: I sleep. sugar stays.
on Ann Street, I pluck tight strings and forget
the hot slash of your name. my mother salts

a hard-boiled egg. my sister catches salt
water on a toothbrush from the sink. bagged
celery stalks. black nose hairs. I forget
how grief chases the pink mouth,
tussles with the teeth. begs to stay.

in the neighborhood, recyclables stay
in green bins. fathers stay, too: cast cubes of salt
onto driveways. we are flush with snow. mouths
of dogs flip open. our pink tongues hang. I bag
grief between two slices of white bread. I forget

with every bite. you died. you died. forget-
ful, hoarse, I try calling you back. grief brays. I stay
inside the house with yellow lights. I eat a bag
full of candies with my fist. once, salt
slid across your tongue and you mouthed

the words to a Joni Mitchell song: *a mouth
like yours*—I had a mouth. it was yours. I forget
all the noisy ways you were mine, scattered like salt

across a table. my mouth sticks. grief stays.
outside, birds swallow; you crumble. I shut the bag.

AND WHEN

you ask your legs to chase after it: orange
light. rubber band. smashed aluminum cans
by the gutter. in rain, in heat: your thighs lift
and lift. climb the dusty stairs. pull apart
the bread with your wrists. know
what you are asking for: for the grief to touch
you on the backs of your knees. for the grief
to chase through the skull, popping into
a shiny mouth.   run, girl, run.
imagine you are a shark. bare your shark teeth.
you are pointed and sharp: strong. here are biceps.
here is a reef. here is what you have lost: fish
tanks full of tiny fins and tails. places
you could have gone: blurry, now. here is
what you miss: red marks on your neck
from where the first love watered with his mouth.
snare drums you did not learn how to play.
smokes you did not press between your lips.
you could have had so much: grief
grills into the shoulder blades. terrible
and stunning and wet.   run, girl, run.
here are your shoelaces: here is the rain.
here is what dazzles you, still: apple cores.
a stranger on the bus. his puffy mouth.
run, girl, run.   run, girl, run.
you are a shark. aren't you
a shark? where are

your fins? lift up.
bare your teeth.
press all you have
to the good dirt.
open wide
open: in
comes
the grief
as you
pound
your legs,
as you
toss a tail.
the air
is humid
and small
with loss.

shark, girl, shark.

do not be
afraid to
bite.

I WANT MY BOOKS BACK

I want your shirt on. I want
your arms clasped behind
your back, your dumb skull
off my pillow. I want you
to untouch my hair in May,
when we ate chicken from
a paper box and somewhere,
cars scattered gold-red light
across our cheeks, gravel.
I want no petal, no tongue,
no car ride with the roof
down, slinging Aretha
Franklin 'til the front seat
vibrated. I want no sun.
I want none of your dog
licking me with her snout,
her tender hair on a leash.
I want no Thanksgiving
in bed, video game buttons
beneath our clean finger-
nails; I want to stop
shooting pirates
with guns. I want
each letter I wrote
to unwrite itself, return
to my body as black
alphabet, 3:00 a.m. lamp-

light, taste of licorice
and loss; I want to eat
the envelopes back up.
I want you gobbled by lion-
fish; I want you puddle,
then melt; I want you ghost,
ghost, ghost again;
I want you to say it:
Sorry, love. Love, I
am so sorry, then grieve
the going of me,
the way you would
a spilled can
of cream. I want
the wind to stop,
the salt to pelt.
I want the birds
to keep blowing.
I want to tie my
shoes, one string
laid against
the other, then
pull—taut—violently
with my hands;
I want to yank
you out.

ZODIAC

on the porch, we eat hard-boiled
eggs with salt, and watch thumb-
tacks strike the hardwood floors.

I tell you you're pretty.
you push your tongue
into the yolks.

you ask me for your zodiac sign.

on the porch, my black hair
seethes, and I open my mouth,
wobble. Mom said, *American
girls talk too much.* I press a
finger to my lip. somewhere,
a butterfly grates wings against
the rocks. I hold the trowel.

I'm part American, part
rooster. in sun, your blond
hairs warble. I admire your
minty neck, nails. I envy
you. how the English laces
inside your tidy throat.

Mom warned, *Be
polite.* I spread—trill

my feathers—you
jump; I claw. eggshells
topple from our laps.

WÁNXIÀO: the chicken words for *joke*.

you watch and I snap
my throat. I cry
at the break of day.
I demand morning,
the pinkest sun,
clouds scraping
against a skinny sky,

my beak tilted
upward like
a flag.

YEARS

I drink coffee and learn it is
a laxative. toilet seats. ice cubes.
songs that remind me of you:
songs that don't. the rain is
a silver tambourine over
my head. in every class I
teach I begin with a proverb.
birds, pots of gold. *No man is
an island.* I ask my Malaysian
students to define *glitter.*
they make a shaking motion
with their hands. in Japan,
I meet a white-haired woman who
tells me her name means *moon.*
But I am crescent now, she says.
Soon I will disappear. we wave
to each other on the subway.
the chairs are plastic
and blue. I forget my watch,
and the map winks with lines.
easy. the thousand ways I sit.
bound for Nasu, I watch
a mother swipe her child
on the cheek. in me: muscle,
bone. my sister's nose, my father's
tongue. the way he says *prawn.*
the way I wash a well-oiled

platter. the way I kiss
another mouth. pears.
pearls. I bite. I bite.
somebody pours
water into the mug: perfect
downfall. wet, bluing
squiggles. forget
subways. forget
I called. when I ascend
the stairs I see a cat
near a stray mango tree. I
do not shy away. I say my own
name. plug my fist into
the jar of honey, electrify.
disappear, then come
home again. tomorrow
I'll eat. and the years
will turn themselves over.
milk, spirals
of rain. what we
choose. worlds we
kiss. everything
we leave behind—
wrappers. shadows.
a mammal, howling beneath
the streetlight. licking
her own ancient skin.

PICKING RASPBERRIES WITH ADAM

—*i.*

red juice sliding over a thumb / & no sign
telling us we can't eat / so we eat
'til bees slip past / all of us giddy
rocked in red / winged with sugar

Adam holds up a branch / I let the red
fall & fall / into me / like surf

four months left / before I

                                 leave / beg
                                 what I love / to stay.

—*ii.*

already, the branch / slumps
curvy with red / and Adam
talks about / lunar cycles
silver bracelets / Catherine's
Taiwanese grandma / regal
in her praise / of Adam's hair
I want to press / my bold head
to the ground / scoop up
berry after berry / then lose
count / tell the dirt to
remember me / & these
hands / which prayed
in the dark / after tasting
berries stuck / to its snout.

—iii.

we fill the plastic jugs / tied
to our waists / & drive past
stalks of corn / that remind me
of my crush's shoulders / tall
& generous & lean / I am
surprised at how / it takes me
years to forget / the way my
father called, once / said,
You are very amazing / while at
home my mother / boiled
ears of yellow corn / which
we ate / sitting down / hot
& wordless / with wonder.

—iv.

driving home / with Adam
raspberries / in the backseat
I am reminded of
what I'll leave behind:

        magnets on a fridge
        & white stems
        & the same silver pan
        I washed / for years
        before learning / it came
        from my mother's mother.

        & here, when I thought I knew
        everything / so eager to leave—

the metallic touch / of
these women / pulled
some muscle / in me
spun my chest / red
new longing for / hands
& dirt / cool walks / rice

here go / constant surprises
even in a space / I thought I owned.

—*v.*

the truth is / I want to leave
but I don't want to leave
& I know nothing / & everything, still
praise today / berry juice / a friend / the time

on we go / the bushes laced / with bees
while the days roll by
magnificent / shiny / strong

at the curb I tell Adam / good-bye
& I love all I love / with my wide
open mouth / I bite down
bite down / & keep biting
I don't / spit any of it / out.

PLEDGE 2.0, TRIBE, ZOO

I get up I eat I rinse my mouth I squeeze
the juice I play with hair all of it mine
all of it a cape—black—chasing freckles down
my neck chasing freckles down the tender
back outside a bee shimmers
past, my knees crack, the grass and its
sharp green flags the woman and her
sharp green laugh I pledge allegiance
to the grass of the United States of America
I pledge allegiance to breath, one nation,
hills and hills of skin the body for which
I stand my own animal my own paws
in the grocery aisle I claim plums like stars
look at me black haired
and bursting I have black hair
on my fist these are my arms
this is my nation look at me
I look at you bless all of this
looking, crooking
under eye after starry
eye, indivisible

two tongued.

ACKNOWLEDGMENTS

Endless praise for all the gracious brains and breaths who have made this book possible.

Thank you to the editors of these journals, who generously gave the following poems a place to nest before they made their way into this book:

Room: "Hey, Man"

Bodega: "Picking Raspberries with Adam"

Sugared Water: "When All You Want," "Then I Woke Up in Your Bed"

Berkeley Poetry Review: "Morning Comes, I Am Shiny with It"

Tinderbox Poetry Journal: "Your Mom Tells You to Stop Writing About Race," "Calumet," "Years"

The *Margins*: "Letting the Dogs Out" (previously "Ann Arbor, Michigan • Generation 1"), "When I Boiled the Corn"

Stirring: "Everything's a Fly"

Thank you, too, to the National Federation of State Poetry Societies, which selected and published the following poems as a part of its 2015 Edna Meudt Memorial Award–winning chapbook:

"I Wasn't Joking," "What You Lookin' At, Chink?," "Here I Go, Torching," "Severed," and "Game Boy Advance."

To my many brilliant teachers from the University of Michigan and Ann Arbor communities—Jeremiah Chamberlin, Anne Curzan, John Whittier-Ferguson, Dee Matthews, Keith Taylor, Cody Walker, and Amy Sara Carroll—thank you, truly. You raise me and challenge me to grow. To Nate Marshall, for seeing me, for teaching me, for making me laugh. To Jeff Kass, for remaining a steadfast hero and friend. To Morgan Parker, for your faith in these words, and your careful & courageous eye. And to all the kind folks at Little A—Vivian Lee and the entire team—thank you for making this book come to fruition. I am so grateful.

My thanks to these fine souls, who lift me—this book has wings because of you: Yaoyao Liu, Teresa Mathew, Harleen Kaur, Jasmine An, Aaron Noffke, Haley Smith, Bianca Patel, Hope Kassen, Kacy Rauschenberger, Hanifa Sariman, Molly Williams, Blaise Bennardo, Lillian Li, Margaret Grumeretz, Justin Younan, Adam DesJardins, Catherine Tao, Alex Winnick, Khanh San Pham, Anna Burch, Cheng and Yue Li, Jenny Shen, Gahl Liberzon, Alex Kime, Fiona Chamness, Clara Kaul, Jaime Davidson, Löwe Denken Wir, Eliza Cadoux, Danielle Flanders, Jean Rafaelian, and too many more to name. Love supreme.

A huge shout-out to the Neutral Zone, Volume Youth Poetry Project, and Red Beard Press: best spaces in the nation, home, and heart; you taught me first. Love to Michigan in Color for showing me how to listen. Ann Arbor Wordworks family: you fueled the poet and sister I aim to be. Thank you to my students, particularly the Red Beard Press 2014 and 2015 crews, and 4A and 5B at SMK Jengka 16. From you, I learn so much.

I am grateful for every single stage or page that has ever welcomed a poem of mine and for every giant heart that has ever paused to listen.

To my *năinai*, to my *wàigōng*. To my Qingdao family. To Karen, to my parents: love, love, love again. And every day, thank you, with every muscle I am. In English, *Zhōngwén*, Chinglish, no matter how we say it—I am so proud to be yours.

ABOUT THE AUTHOR

Carlina Duan hails from Ann Arbor, Michigan, where she earned her BA from the University of Michigan. As a 2016 Fulbright grant recipient, she lived and taught in Malaysia before returning to the States to pursue work as a literary arts educator and freelancer. Her poems have been anthologized and published in *Uncommon Core*, *Tinderbox Poetry Journal*, *The Margins*, and *Berkeley Poetry Review*, among others. *I Wore My Blackest Hair* is her first full-length poetry collection. She is currently an MFA candidate at Vanderbilt University.